Europe

A Buddy Book
by
Cheryl Striveildi

ABDO
Publishing Company

VISIT US AT
www.abdopub.com

Published by Buddy Books, an imprint of ABDO Publishing Company, 4940 Viking Drive, Edina, Minnesota 55435. Copyright © 2003 by Abdo Consulting Group, Inc. International copyrights reserved in all countries. No part of this book may be reproduced in any form without written permission from the publisher.

Printed in the United States.

Edited by: Christy DeVillier
Contributing Editors: Matt Ray, Michael P. Goecke
Graphic Design: M. Hosley
Image Research: Deborah Coldiron
Photographs: Corbis, Corel, Fotosearch, Photodisc, PhotoEssentials

Library of Congress Cataloging-in-Publication Data

Striveildi, Cheryl, 1971-
    Continents. Europe / Cheryl Striveildi.
        p. cm.
    Includes index.
    Summary: A very brief introduction to the geography, climate, plants, and animals of Europe.
        ISBN 1-57765-962-7
            1. Europe—Juvenile literature. 2. Europe—Geography—Juvenile literature. [1. Europe.] I. Title: Europe. II. Title.

D1051 .S84 2003
940—dc21

                                                                2002074663

Table of Contents

Seven Continents

Water covers most of the earth. Land covers the rest. The earth has seven main land areas, or **continents**. The seven continents are:

 North America

 Africa

 South America

 Asia

 Europe

 Australia

 Antarctica

Europe is full of beautiful sights.

Europe is the second-smallest continent. It covers about 3,837,400 square miles (9,938,000 sq km).

Europe is not much bigger than the United States. Yet, this continent is full of beautiful sights. Europe has great castles, churches, and other landmarks. Europe's art and food are world famous, too.

Where Is Europe?

A **hemisphere** is half of the earth. Europe is in the Northern Hemisphere.

The Atlantic Ocean lies between Europe and North America. The Arctic Ocean is north of Europe. The Mediterranean Sea and the Black Sea lie south of Europe.

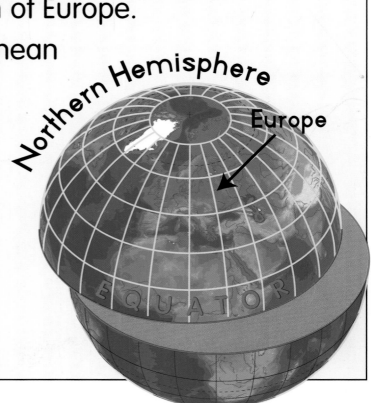

Northern Hemisphere

Europe

EQUATOR

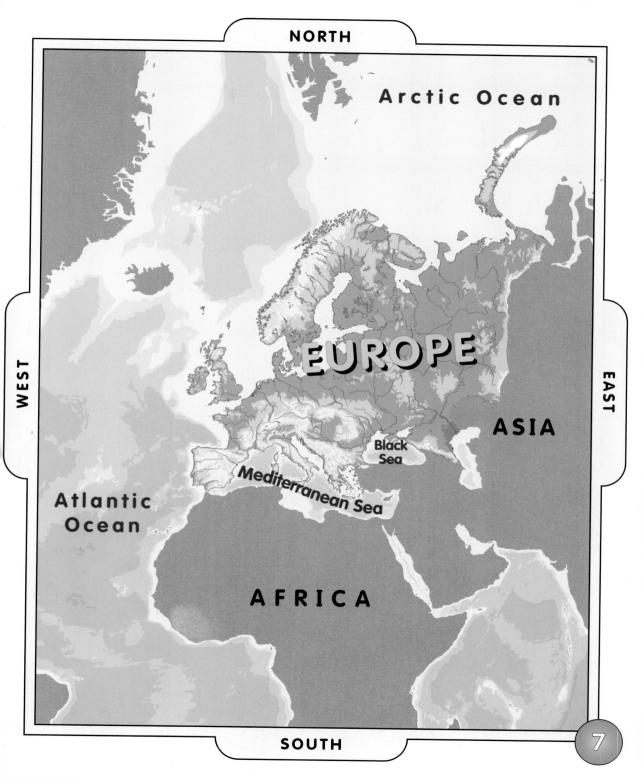

Asia is east of Europe. In fact, these two **continents** are joined together. Some people call the landmass of Europe and Asia "Eurasia." But most people believe they are separate continents. This is because Europe and Asia are very different.

The Ural Mountains, the Caspian Sea, and the Black Sea are on Europe's border. They separate Europe and Asia.

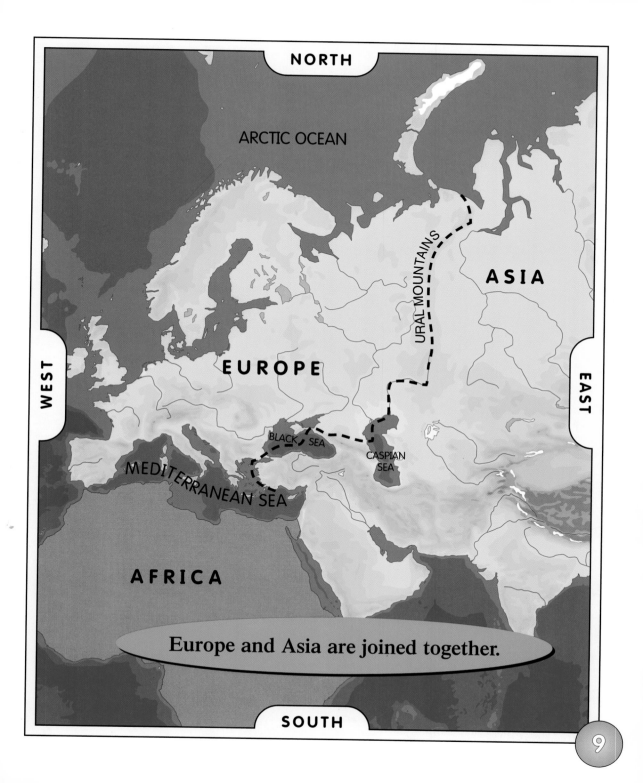

NORTH

ARCTIC OCEAN

ASIA

URAL MOUNTAINS

EUROPE

WEST

EAST

BLACK SEA

CASPIAN SEA

MEDITERRANEAN SEA

AFRICA

Europe and Asia are joined together.

SOUTH

9

Countries

There are 47 countries in Europe. The people of each country have their own **customs**. Food, holidays, and language often change from country to country. More than 50 different languages are spoken in Europe. Many Europeans speak more than one language.

Netherlands

Italy

Switzerland

Germany

Four of the 47 countries in Europe.

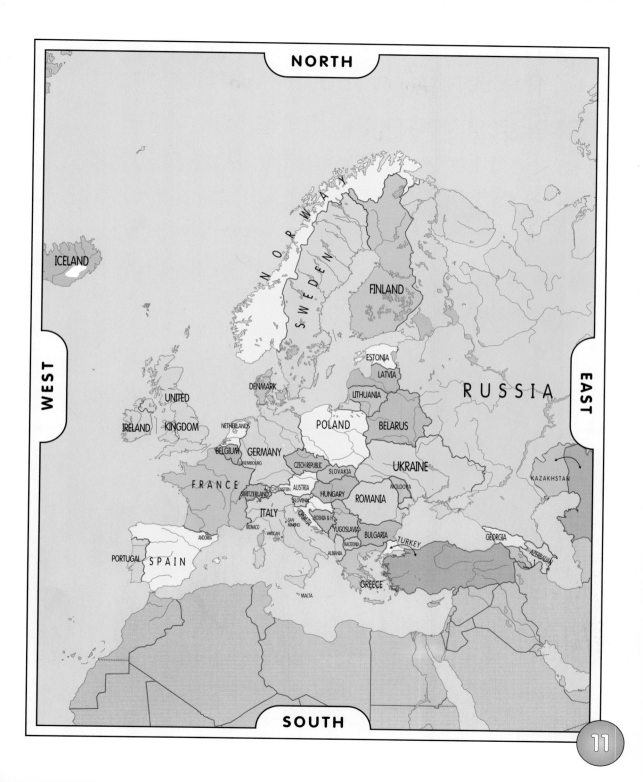

ICELAND

N O R W A Y

S W E D E N

FINLAND

ESTONIA

LATVIA

DENMARK

LITHUANIA

RUSSIA

UNITED
KINGDOM

NETHERLANDS

POLAND

BELARUS

IRELAND

BELGIUM

GERMANY

LUXEMBOURG

CZECH REPUBLIC

SLOVAKIA

UKRAINE

KAZAKHSTAN

FRANCE

LIECHTENSTEIN

AUSTRIA

SWITZERLAND

SLOVENIA

HUNGARY

MOLDOVA

ROMANIA

ITALY

CROATIA

BOSNIA & H.

SAN
MARINO

MONACO

VATICAN
CITY

YUGOSLAVIA

BULGARIA

GEORGIA

PORTUGAL

SPAIN

ANDORRA

MACEDONIA

TURKEY

AZERBAIJAN

ALBANIA

GREECE

MALTA

The European country with the most people is Germany. But Russia is the biggest European country. Part of Russia is in Asia, too.

Russia is the biggest country in the world.

St. Peter's Basilica is a famous church in Vatican City.

Vatican City is the smallest European country. Only about 1,000 people live there. Vatican City lies within the Italian city of Rome.

British Isles

Many islands make up the British Isles. They lie in the Atlantic Ocean off Europe's northwest coast. Among these islands are Ireland, the Shetlands, and the Isle of Man. The biggest one is Great Britain. Together, Scotland, Wales, and England make up the island of Great Britain.

A country home in Great Britain

London is a city in England. This city is hundreds of years old. One famous **landmark** in London is Buckingham Palace. Buckingham Palace is home to the queen of England and her family.

Buckingham Palace

The Alps

The Alps lie in France, Italy, Switzerland, Austria, Germany, and Slovenia. This mountain chain is about 600 miles (966 km) long. Many people like to hike and ski in the Alps.

The Alps

The Alps have cliffs, meadows, and forests.

Many wild animals live in the Alps. There are small animals like squirrels and marmots. There are bigger animals like deer, chamois, and ibex. An ibex is a wild goat. Lynx and wildcats live there, too.

Ibex

Squirrel

There are villages in the Alps.

People live in the Alps, too. Some villages have less than 200 people. One Swiss village is called Gimmelwald. This tiny village has no cars, newspapers, or food stores. To get there, people must walk or take a cable car.

The Mediterranean

Many European countries border the Mediterranean Sea. These countries have hot summers and rainy winters. The Mediterranean **climate** is good for growing fruits.

A ship in the Mediterranean Sea

Olives grow on trees.

Olives grow in Spain, Italy, and Greece. Most of the world's olive oil comes from these countries. Olive oil is an important part of Mediterranean cooking.

Grapes grow in many Mediterranean countries, too. Some grapes are used to make wine. France, Spain, and Italy are famous for their wines.

Wine is made from grapes.

Northern Europe

The winters are very cold in northern Europe. No trees grow in the far north. This land is **tundra**. The tundra stays mostly frozen.

No trees can grow on the tundra.

Iceland is an island in the Atlantic Ocean. Parts of Iceland have big, icy **glaciers**. These glaciers sometimes cover 4,500 square miles (11,655 sq km).

Glaciers move slowly across land.

"White nights" happen when the sun does not go down.

Parts of northern Europe have "white nights." This is when the sun shines through the night. These bright nights happen in the summertime. In Iceland, "white nights" last for two or three months.

Northern Lights

In the far north, people can see the northern lights. These natural lights sometimes light up the night sky. The northern lights look like streaks or clouds of colorful light. They may be green, purple, or red.

Visiting Europe

France is the biggest country of western Europe. France's capital city is Paris. Paris is hundreds of years old. It is on the Seine River.

Paris and the Seine River

People visiting Europe commonly stop in Paris. This French city has many landmarks. Two of them are the Eiffel Tower and the Arc de Triomphe. Paris is also famous for fine food and art. One of Paris's great art museums is the Louvre.

Arc de Triomphe

The Eiffel Tower is a famous European landmark.

Europe

- Europe is the second-smallest continent.

- Europe's highest point is the top of Mount Elbrus.

- Russia is Europe's biggest country. The smallest European country is Vatican City.

- Great Britain is the eighth-biggest island in the world.

- Europe's lowest point is the Caspian Sea.

- More than 700 million people live in Europe.

Important Words

climate the rain, wind, and temperature of a place over time.

continent one of the earth's seven main land areas.

customs the way of life common to a group of people. Language, food, clothes, and religion are customs.

glacier a huge chunk of ice and snow on land.

hemisphere one half of the earth.

landmark a famous building or place.

tundra flat land with no trees in the far north.

Web Sites

Would you like to learn more about Europe?
Please visit ABDO Publishing Company on the World Wide Web to find web site links about Europe.
These links are routinely monitored and updated to provide the most current information available.

www.abdopub.com

Index